A spiritual manifesto
for a better way of life

THE
SLAVE

A spiritual manifesto for a better way of life

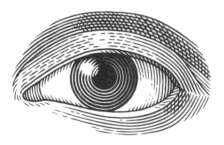

ANAND DÍLVAR

HAY HOUSE

Carlsbad, California • New York City • London
Sydney •Johannesburg • Vancouver • New Delhi

Published and distributed in the United States of America by:
Shelter Harbor Press, 603 W. 115th Street, Suite 163, New York, NY 10025

First published and distributed in the United Kingdom by:
Hay House UK Ltd, Astley House, 33 Notting Hill Gate, London W11 3JQ
Tel: +44 (0)20 3675 2450; Fax: +44 (0)20 3675 2451; www.hayhouse.co.uk

Published and distributed in India by:
Hay House Publishers India, Muskaan Complex, Plot No.3, B-2,
Vasant Kunj, New Delhi 110 070
Tel: (91) 11 4176 1620; Fax: (91) 11 4176 1630; www.hayhouse.co.in

A catalogue record for this book is available from the British Library.

ISBN: 978-1-78817-150-2

Printed and bound by CPI Group (UK) Ltd, Croydon, CR0 4YY

CONTENTS

"The hardest thing is to die and be reborn."
BUDDHA

"I came to the understanding that this life is the only opportunity we have to be ourselves."
THE SLAVE

PROLOGUE

THIS IS A BOOK WORTH READING AND THEN RE-READING A FEW TIMES. Its language is pleasantly forthright; the story is genuine. Who has not been, or isn't still, a slave to problems, fears, and guilt? The author guides us quickly and simply through the universe of the mind to where we can find our healthy Self, whom it seems we can hear only when we ourselves cannot speak.

Anand Dílvar has enriched the knowledge he acquired in the Gestalt University of America with his experiences on long journeys throughout Asia, and especially in India.

The character in this book represents us. Through him, we come to understand that by trying to escape our reality through alcohol or drugs, we blind ourselves to the miracles that surround us. Through him, we also come to understand that we do not value what we have until it is lost.

This book will keep you, dear reader, in a constant state of suspense. Once you pick it up, you will not be able to put it down.

It is an ode to life.

DR HÉCTOR SALAMA PENHOS
Director of the Gestalt University of America

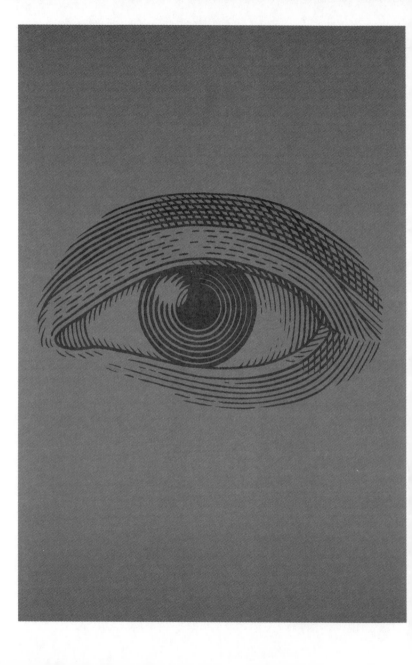

CHAPTER I

WHEN I CAME TO, I REALIZED RIGHT AWAY THAT SOMETHING WAS VERY WRONG.

A blinding light was hurting my eyes, but I couldn't blink. I tried to look away, to move my arms and cover my face with my hands, but I could not.

My whole body was paralyzed, racked with excruciating pain, and colder than I had ever felt.

I tried to call out, to cry for help, but it was useless. There was something in my mouth that made my throat burn, and a terrible noise thundered in my ears.

Several hours went by, and my mind whirled with desperation. From despair I slowly progressed to terror, as a few coherent thoughts managed to filter through the pain in my head . . .

Where am I?
What's happening to me?
I must be dead . . .

The mixture of pain, dread, and these ominous thoughts made me pass out, thank God, giving me a little respite.

I don't know if hours or days went by before I woke up again.

I was still unable to move, with my eyes wide open. The pain had lessened a little and the light still dazzled my eyes, but it was more bearable. It was then that I realized that the awful noise I heard was a kind of labored breathing, deep and heavy … it was not my breath, of that I was sure.

That my physical torment had let up slightly opened the door to a whole new kind of suffering: mental confusion and a sudden urgent need for answers.

Am I really dead?
Who is that I hear breathing?
What's this thing in my mouth that's hurting my throat?

Little by little, memories of what I thought was the day before came flashing back—the party, drinks, the argument with Laura, and Edward insisting that I try that stupid drug he was so excited about.

"Please stop drinking! Can't you see you're killing yourself?" Laura was shouting at me. "Is that what you want?"
"I don't want to die—I just want to escape."
"Escape from what? You're crazy."
"Yeah, I'm crazy and you don't understand me! Nobody does …"

I tossed into my mouth the two blue pills I had accepted from Edward. That was the last thing I remembered.

Oh, my God! I finally managed it! I've killed myself.
This can't be happening! What's wrong with me? Why can't
I move? Why can't I close my eyes?
That idiot poisoned me, I thought. *And now I'm in Hell*
paying for what I did … It's even worse than I would've
imagined.

I wasn't a great believer in life after death, but at that moment there seemed to be no other explanation.

Please, God! Please forgive me! Give me another chance …

The sound of a door opening interrupted my train of thought. I heard a woman's voice:

"What a racket that piece of trash makes!" she said.
"It's the only one we have. You know what this place
is like," replied a man.
"How is it possible that we only have one artificial
respiration unit?"
"Well, that's how it is. We just have to do the best we
can."
"So what happened to him?"

"*He* is really screwed. Why don't you uncover him and take a look?"

I felt a sheet being pulled back from my face and could see a woman in a white uniform who stared at me with an expression of startled fright.

"He's awake!"

The man standing next to her leaned over to see better.

"No, he was like that when they brought him in. When they dropped him off at ER they said he'd had an accident, but he was high as a kite. Still conscious, though; kept saying 'Laura, I'm sorry' over and over again. After that he went into a coma and he seems to have something like a kind of rigor mortis—we couldn't get his eyes to close."
"Poor devil! He'd be better off dead."
"You mean *we'd* be better off! Now we have a vegetable to keep alive, in a bed that somebody else needs. What a waste of electricity!"
"Do you think he can see or hear … or feel anything?"
"Of course not, watch this …"

I saw a tube moving close to the bed and felt a stab of

pain in my arm.

That hurts, you jerk! I'm alive … I'm awake! Help me!!!

I tried uselessly to scream.

"You might as well change his drip, now that we're here," the man said. "Someone's got to water the vegetables!"

They both chuckled and a wave of rage and desperation washed over me.

The man left the room. The woman changed a bottle that was hanging next to the bed and quickly followed him out.

So now I had some answers. I replayed the conversation in my mind:

"An accident …"
"Went into a coma …"
"Laura, I'm sorry …"
"Someone's got to water the vegetables …
"… water the vegetables …"
"… the vegetables …"

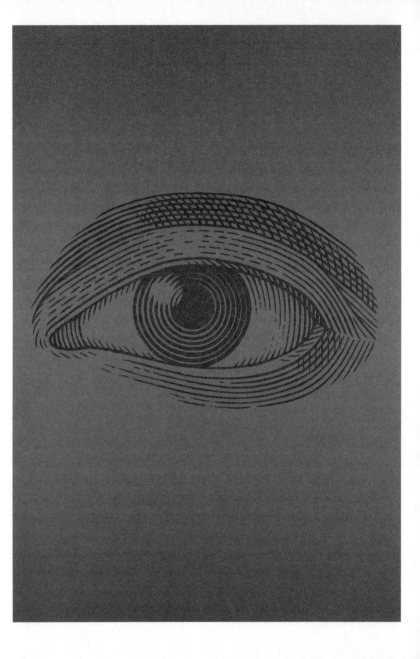

CHAPTER II

IN THE FIRST FEW DAYS, I MANAGED TO EXPLORE THE ROOM I WAS IN A LITTLE. THAT IS TO SAY, I EXPLORED THE PART OF THE ROOM THAT WAS WITHIN MY IMMOBILE FIELD OF VISION.

Above me was a tatty, neon ceiling lamp that looked as if it was about to fall down.

To the right of the bed was a hook for my drip, which the nurse came in to change once a day. Further over to the right I could make out a tube containing a black, bellows-like pump that rose and fell in time with what I had now come to think of as "my breathing."

To my left there was a complicated-looking machine with switches, lights, and displays. I later found out that this was responsible for controlling my respiration, my heart rate, and the nutrients being administered through a tube going into my stomach.

Behind that machine I could see part of a window, which was the source of much of my torment: the light that came in through the window every morning hurt my eyes, waking me up and bringing me back to the living hell I was in.

The physical pain was nothing compared to the mental

torture that my own mind inflicted on me. Helplessness, guilt, anger, fear, and the impossibility of expressing any of these emotions combined in my head to drive me insane.

Every day, I wished to not wake up again, that the machine keeping me alive would break down and put an end to my suffering.

What gave these doctors the right to keep me here? What possible use was there in keeping me alive? I was a damned vegetable, unable to move or speak!

I was overcome by impotence, which began to curdle into hatred. Hatred for the people who were keeping me alive, hatred of life itself.

The nurse was right: I would be better off dead. And yet, every day she came into my room with her scared expression to change the drip that was feeding me. Even though she believed me to be unconscious, she never looked me in the eye. She would hurriedly check that all the tubes between my body and the machine were all right, and rush out as soon as she could.

Each day, when I saw her arrive, I would mentally plead with her to not take care of me. Didn't she realize that she wasn't doing me any favors by keeping me alive?

Please, leave that alone! I would beseech her in my mind. *If you're too afraid to look at me, why don't you just stop coming? Just let me die …*

But again and again I was forced to watch as she went through her routine, leaving me here … alive. Again and again and again …

God damn it! I wish this was over!

Please, somebody do something! Somebody help me! I don't want to live anymore!

"You'd better get used to it. Looks like you're going to be there for a while," I suddenly heard a voice say to me, despite the fact that there was no one else in the room.

"You really screwed up this time, didn't you?" the strange voice went on.

Who are you? An angel? I replied, frightened. Somehow I understood that the voice was not coming from outside of me.

"Ha! You're the world's biggest atheist and now you believe in God and angels? Come on!"

How can you tell what I'm thinking? Have I gone mad?

"That's a distinct possibility."

So you're not real?

"Look, I really can't tell you anything that you don't already know … Maybe later you'll realize who I am."

Laura … Is she okay? Why haven't my parents been to see me? When am I going to die? Is this my punishment?

"Don't be so damned blockheaded! I told you I don't

know anything that you don't."

In that case, you're not much use to me.

"If you want, I'll leave."

No!!! Please don't go.

That's when I remembered that Laura used to talk all the time about spirit guides. She thought that if you meditated enough you could communicate with them, although personally I thought that was a load of crap.

"I think so too, although I must say I like this 'guide' thing," replied the voice.

Was it possible for a spiritual guide to be this sarcastic and rude?

"Look, buddy, if you don't like me, I'll leave and that will be that."

No, no. Don't get mad, I'm just trying to understand what's going on.

"Maybe you should've tried that before you went and got yourself into this mess in the first place."

I was just trying to escape, to get away from my problems!

"Right! You wanted to get away from your problems and you made yourself a slave."

A slave?

"You have no free will, you can't move or talk. You

couldn't even kill yourself if you wanted to."

And you just came along to make me feel even worse about myself?

"I just 'came along'? I've always been here; the problem is that you never wanted to listen to me before. Besides, nobody can make you feel anything."

That's just stupid. What do you mean nobody can make me feel anything? My mom and dad always made me angry, my brother and sisters made me feel inferior, my girlfriends were constantly letting me down and hurting me.

"Let me explain. Before you ended up in here, you were as free as a bird. Nobody and nothing had any power over you. You could have done absolutely anything. You were in control of your own life."

What does any of that have to do with my feelings?

"You in some kind of a rush? We have more than enough time to think things over and talk at leisure …"

You're one son-of-a-bitch!

"You were also free to think whatever you wanted, and so to choose the way you felt."

Choose the way I felt?

"That's right. Your feelings come from, and can only come from, your thoughts. Here's how it works: you think about something sad and you feel sad. You think about something that annoys you and you feel angry. You think that other people can hurt you or disappoint you or make you feel bad, but really no one can get inside your mind and make you think or feel anything. Even right now, when other people could move your body around and do whatever they like with it, or turn off the machine keeping you alive, you're still in control of your mind."

I thought you said you couldn't tell me anything I didn't already know.

"Well, that's the only thing that proves you're not as stupid as you thought."

What?

"You were always blaming other people and circumstances for the things that went wrong in your life. You were a victim."

Well, yeah. My life wasn't easy, you know. I mean, just look at the family I got, and then I always had bad luck.

"Aw, poor little you! When you think like that you're a slave to your past, to other people's desires, to circumstance, and to luck."

So I was supposed to control everything that went on? I was supposed to control other people?

"You can't control circumstances but you can control your reaction to circumstances. You were and still are in control of what happens inside your mind. You are the one who decides what thoughts to have and how to react to a situation."

Yeah, right. How was I supposed to react positively to all the problems I had?

"You had the choice to look at them as problems or as obstacles to be overcome, as a curse or a challenge. If it wasn't up to you to decide how to react, then who?"

Okay, now you're making me mad. You're saying that the only person responsible for everything bad that happens to me is ME?

"YOU'RE making yourself mad. Besides, it's not about blaming anyone. But just tell me … who moved your hand that time you hit Laura? Who was moving your hand when you helped yourself to one drink after another? Who put those pills in your mouth that landed you in here?"

I felt about to explode. I suppose that expressing emotions is a kind of safety valve, and I couldn't even cry. I was furious at what my "guide" was telling me, but the worst thing about it was that he was absolutely right about everything.

Luckily, at that moment something happened to distract my attention: the door opened and a nurse came in. It wasn't the sour-faced woman who usually changed my drip. She came to the bed and bent over to get a look at me.

I could see a great deal of sadness in her green eyes. Her blonde hair kept falling over her face and she was constantly tucking it behind her ears. She scrutinized me for a few seconds and I managed to get a look at her hospital name tag: Faith.

"Hi," she said.

Hi, Faith, I imagined myself saying back.

"Look at the state you're in, you poor thing."

Oh, you know, that's life, I continued with the conversation in my head.

She stroked my hair and said, "Don't worry, I'll look after you."

Thanks, I thought.

"You know, she's a LOT closer to being an angel than I am," said my guide. "And she's also cute!"

She carefully changed my drip, rearranged the pillows under my head, and checked that the machines around me were working as they should.

"See you tomorrow," she said as she turned to leave.

See you tomorrow, I answered.

"See you tomorrow, hot stuff!!!" yelled my guide in my head.

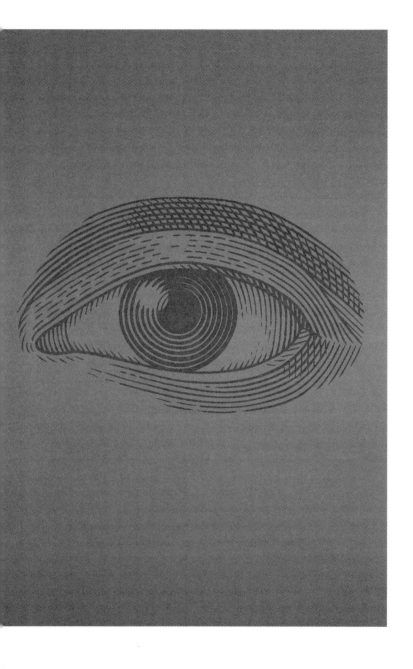

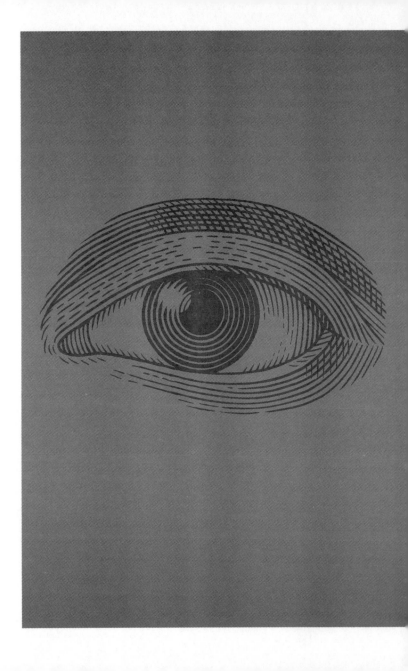

CHAPTER III

THAT NIGHT I HAD A STRANGE DREAM. I WAS A WOODEN PUPPET WITH STRINGS RUNNING TO MY FEET, HANDS, AND HEAD. ON THE OTHER END OF THE STRINGS, SEVERAL PEOPLE WERE TAKING TURNS TO MAKE ME MOVE: I SAW MY PARENTS, A TEACHER OR TWO, THE PRIEST FROM MY CHURCH, AND AN EX-GIRLFRIEND. THEY WERE ALL HAVING A GREAT TIME, LAUGHING AND MAKING ME JUMP AND DANCE ABOUT, PUTTING ME IN RIDICULOUS POSITIONS AND MAKING ME GESTICULATE LIKE A CHIMPANZEE.

In my dream I knew that I could easily break the strings but preferred to let myself be manipulated. It was comfortable, easy, something I'd grown to know. I realized that this was my conditioning, to let other people make my decisions rather than take responsibility for myself.

When they were all tired of playing with me, they left me in a heap on the floor. The floor became a bed and I could see the ceiling lamp in my room. I had woken up.

Sleeping with my eyes wide open was the weirdest thing; it was hard to get to sleep at night and in the mornings it was sometimes difficult to tell where my dreams ended and reality began. I sometimes knew I was dreaming because I could move and was no longer in that horrible hospital room. Then I would run as fast and as far away as possible and would wish never to wake up; but day after day I found myself looking at the lamp, the ceiling, the black bellows moving up and down, and the machine keeping me in that never-ending nightmare.

The door opened and Faith came in. She was carrying a plastic container with water in it.

"Good morning!" she said brightly.
Good morning, I answered, as usual.
"Today is bath day."
Oh, God, no! Please, how embarrassing!

She pulled the sheet off me and took off the white hospital gown that covered my naked body. I was burning up with helplessness and shame. I really was the puppet I had dreamt about and other people really could do whatever they liked with me.

But something in her eyes calmed me down. I suppose that instead of seeing a naked man, she saw just another patient like the many others she cared for every day.

She moistened a sponge in the water and began to wipe my face.

"Look at you, you're so young."

Why did she talk to me? Did she know I could hear her?

"You're not ugly either," she said smiling coyly and blushing a little. "I hope you're not conscious, you poor thing."

I'm conscious!!!

"I hope you're gone already and the only thing left is your body."

No, damn it!!! I'm here! I can see you and hear you!

"I guess if you're still in there you must feel pretty lonely."

She was lost in thought for a moment and a tear slowly slid down her cheek.

"I'm lonely too, you know. My husband died a few years ago." She dried her eyes on the sleeve of her white uniform. "Ever since then I've been feeling paralyzed, very afraid and insecure." She kept talking as she sponged my body. "I feel paralyzed by fear, my trauma ..."

You're beautiful, I thought. *And so free.*

"I wish I was braver. I wish I dared to do more. I don't know, go back to university or find another partner, you know, all that stuff."

She finished cleaning me and while she was putting the hospital gown back on me I realized that of all the things I had lost, human contact was what I missed the most. I wanted to ask her not to leave, to keep talking to me a bit.

> "I've got to get back to work, but I'll be back to
> change your drip later."
> *Please don't leave. Stay longer.*

She stroked my hair one last time and looked at me tenderly for a few seconds.

> "I'm sure your family is looking for you and will be in
> to see you soon, John Doe."

She left the room and once again I was alone.

> *John Doe—so they don't know who I am. She was right, I do
> feel alone in here … anonymous and alone … and now I
> understand that it's all my fault.*
> "Guilt is a pointless sentiment." I heard the voice of
> my guide.

I was overjoyed because even though the things he said annoyed me, talking to him was the best way of passing the time in the prison my body had become.

> *Of course, it's all my fault. If I have to accept that I wasn't a*

puppet of circumstance, then the only person to blame for everything that's happened is me!

"This life is full of contradictions; we're born free but we have to work to keep our freedom and we have to accept responsibility for it. Take you: you're alive but at the same time you're not. The doctors think you're suffering from brain death, but you're conscious. Faith, as you realized, has freedom, the possibility to do whatever she wants, but she feels paralyzed just like you."

She said it was because of her trauma.

"The word trauma comes from Greek. It means wound."

Yeah, I read that in a psychology book.

"Of course you read it. If you hadn't, I wouldn't be telling you now. Stop interrupting ... This is the first contradiction in life: human beings are born completely free but totally dependent. In fact, of all the animals, humans are the ones that need the most attention from their parents.

"The child knows that if his parents don't look after him, he'll die. So love becomes a matter of life or death for him.

"Now, when this kid is growing up he doesn't know anything at all. Who do you think he learns everything about life from?"

His parents.

"Exactly. If you arrived on an unknown planet and saw everyone hitting each other, you'd come to the conclusion that was the normal way to behave, right?"

Like that bastard of a father of mine, who used to hit us all.

"Now, the child doesn't know anything about himself either … and who do you think he learns that from?"

From his parents, obviously.

"That's right. The child thinks that these two powerful human beings that his life depends on know everything and are always right. When your father used to tell you 'You're an idiot and good for nothing,' you believed him."

Of course I didn't!

"No? What did you used to say to yourself when you made a mistake?"

I'm such an idiot.

"And what would you say to yourself when you drank again after you'd decided to kick it?"

I'm good for nothing.

"See? Kids also copy the way they relate to everything around them from their parents. If the father thinks that all human beings are bad, the kid will believe it too. If the mother is always worried and anxious, the kid will feel that way too."

That's how we start shackling our hands and feet.

"And it's in this relationship that our traumas, our wounds, begin to form. When you were a little kid and you made a mistake, your dad would insult you and sometimes hit you. You thought you were bad, and this hurt you more than the blows. When your mother told you that if you didn't behave she wouldn't love you any more, she also hurt you and made you feel afraid."

So it's all their fault!

"Listen to what I'm saying! They also have wounds and they did the best they could with the knowledge they had. They also learned from their parents, and their parents from their parents."

It's a vicious circle.

"A circle that can be broken."

Really? It was all new to me but it made so much sense, as if I'd somehow known this all along. I was intrigued. *How?*

"By not looking for someone to blame. Guilt is really just the fear of being rejected by others, a fear based on the fact that when you were little, if your parents rejected you, your life was in danger.

"Your parents used guilt to make you do what they thought was right: 'If you don't eat, you're a bad boy,' 'If you don't behave, I won't love you,' 'People don't like little boys who lie and swear.'"

But it worked!

"Of course it worked. Guilt is an excellent way of controlling other people."

And if there were no guilt we would all do whatever we please, and run around killing each other.

"That just proves my point that guilt is a pointless sentiment because, despite guilt, people still run around killing each other. Where people have failed is in taking responsibility for themselves and their freedom.

"A person who accepts responsibility for his life realizes that he himself makes his own fate and knows that each decision he takes molds his future; he takes responsibility for all his actions but understands that, as he's not perfect, he may make mistakes … and when he does, he doesn't blame himself for it. If it can be fixed, he does something about it; if not, he knows that nothing is going to change regardless of how guilty he feels about what happened.

"Despite all the traumas, despite all the wounds, people always have the choice to make their lives better or to destroy themselves."

People like me? Stop right there. What good is it to me to know this NOW? I'm already lying here a cripple and I have no way to a deal with how angry and sad I am!

"You're still free to choose what you think and how you feel."

*Well right now I choose for you to shut up!!! I choose to feel
sorry for myself, I choose to be sad, hateful, and bitter! If my
parents did the best they could, they really were incompetent!
I was free to do what I wanted with my life and I chose to
drink and take drugs, I chose to end up in here like a goddamn
thinking plant … Today I choose to lose all hope …*

"Those are pretty ugly thoughts."

All I want is to stop thinking and just die!

"Hello, there," said Faith, closing the door behind her.
She walked to the bed and announced, "Great news: it
looks as if your parents finally found you."

No, it can't be them.

"They'll be in later to see you," she said as she changed
the drip. "It's going to be tough for them to see you
like this …"

No, damn it! I don't want them to come.

"Soooo … I thought I'd fix you up a bit." She took a
small comb out of her pocket and started running it
through my hair. Whenever she touched me I felt
myself calm down.

*Why are you doing this? Why do you take such good care of
me when you don't even know me?*

"I'm not much of a religious person," she confided,
"but I do believe that there's a God that looks over
us all."

Oh, sure. That's why He lets me rot in this hell.

"I don't know why bad stuff happens to people," she went on, "but I think God looks after us through people. That's why I'm a nurse: I imagine I'm helping God care for others. I guess sometimes, when they're desperate, people say, 'God, why won't you help me?' But the truth is, God is in the good people that help others out."

She laughed shyly and to me it seemed as if the room lit up. I relaxed and luxuriated in her daily routine with me. It ended too soon.

"There you are. See you next time, Romeo."

She leaned in and gave me a peck on the cheek then hurried out of the room.

The warm glow of love blossoming inside me was cut short by one thought:

My parents are coming!

My guide was right: life is full of contradictions. I miss them so much and at the same time I resent them. I want to see my mother so badly, but I know that to see me like this will cause her a lot of pain.

I hope I can forgive them. I hope they can forgive me. Will Laura be with them?

Night fell as I was still trying to make sense of my mixed feelings about forgiveness, guilt, and resentment until, exhausted, I finally fell asleep.

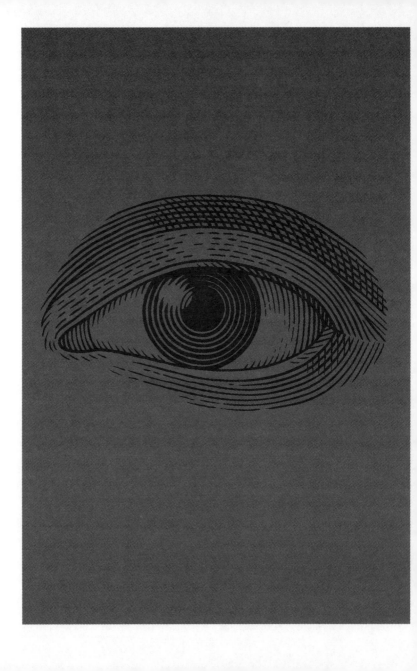

CHAPTER IV

"THERE'S A GOOD BOY, HURRY UP OR YOU'LL
BE LATE FOR SCHOOL."

"Mom, I don't like oatmeal."

"Eat—it'll make you strong so you can study hard and
play with your friends."

*"And so I can ride my bike, because … you're gonna teach
me Saturday, right? Remember you promised?"*

"Of course I do, sweetheart."

I finished my breakfast just as the school bus honked outside.
Mom gave my hair a final brush, checked my uniform, handed
me my lunch box, and kissed me good-bye on the cheek.

I ran to the door and as I opened it the sunlight dazzled me.

Bit by bit my eyes adjusted to the strong light until I finally
could make out my mother's face—not young and carefree like
in the dream I had just awakened from, but aged and grief-
stricken. She kept dabbing at her eyes with a handkerchief.

I also made out my father, standing behind her with his usual
expression of stern fortitude. Not even in a situation like this
would he allow his feelings to show. His consoling hand rested
on my mother's shoulder.

"My son, dear God, answer me!" my mother begged.
"The doctors say he can't hear you. Take it easy," my
father murmured.
"How did this happen to you? Why? Why?" My mother
began to shout and thump on my chest in desperation.

My father pulled her to her feet and held her tight against him
to calm her down.

"Pull yourself together," he implored.
"How can you say that? Look at our son! He's like a
corpse!" she struggled to get away from him.
"This is our fault!" she cried, and fainted away.

My father cradled her in his arms and let her down onto a chair
by the door. He rushed out to get help.

*Mom, I'm sorry! I never meant to cause you pain. This isn't
your fault. You always took care of me and my brother and
sisters.*

She was coming around when my father came hurrying back
with Faith in tow.

"I'll give her a sedative," Faith said. She prepared a
syringe and stuck it in my mother's arm.

"This can't be happening …" my mother kept saying,
as she slumped lifeless in the chair.
"She'll be fine," Faith said, then left.

When I looked at my father, I had never seen him in such a
state. He had lost his composure completely, turning frantically
to my mother in her chair and then to me. His fists were balled
up and his jaw was so tightly clenched I could hear his teeth
grinding. The look in his eyes was the one he used to get when
he was about to hit one of us, and for a moment I was afraid
… but then something happened. All of a sudden he covered
his face with his hands, fell to his knees next to the bed, and
began to sob.

I could hardly believe my eyes. My father had always been
so tough on us. I knew he loved us because we never went
without anything, but it had always been difficult for him to
express his feelings.

He went on crying for what seemed like forever,
occasionally mumbling,

"This isn't possible, this isn't possible …"
"Son, I'm sorry," he finally managed to say, taking my
hand in his. "I love you so much."
I love you, Dad.
"I was so strict with you. I wanted you to have
discipline, to be strong. Now I don't know. I don't
know. Look at you."

I wanted to cry, the sorrow welling up inside me was so very great.

I understand, Dad. I understand now. I know you did the best you could.

"I always hid behind a strongman mask," he went on, "and it's only now with you lying here paralyzed and probably can't even hear me that I can tell you how much I love you. Such a terrible mistake."

I love you too, Dad. I love you too.

My dad let out a heart-wrenching wail.

"I thought if I gave you material stuff, you'd know how much I loved you."

You can't imagine how much I want to give you a hug and a kiss right now, I wished I could say to him.

"It's my fault. I was so hard on you. And the more you fucked up, the harder I got. Maybe I should have been more affectionate. Maybe I should have hugged you more often and demanded less of you. Maybe this is all my fault."

Please, don't keep blaming yourself for this, Dad. I know otherwise now. I know otherwise. I forgive you.

"Maybe it would have been better to try to understand you and talk to you. I'm so sorry."

Still sobbing, he rested his forehead on my chest.

My mother was standing beside him now, staring at him with a puzzled look. She knelt next to him, hugged him, then kissed him on the forehead.

"We have to be strong, honey. God will help us," she said.

They spent the rest of the afternoon at my bedside. They didn't speak, they just looked at each other, and when tears welled up they comforted each other.

The scene reminded me of the time I was in bed with a temperature and they took turns looking after me. Little by little, memories of all the care they had both given me trickled back.

It was thanks to them that I learned to walk and speak. If they hadn't loved me I would never have even survived.

Why only now do I realize how much my parents love me, now that I can't tell them how much I love them and how grateful I am for everything they gave me?

Why did I always blame them for everything that went wrong in my life? Why couldn't I see that they had their own history of joys and sorrows that had molded them to be the way they were?

"You had no compassion," I heard my guide say. "You were so angry at them and blamed them for so many

things that you couldn't see all the good stuff they
gave you.

"When you realize that you're free, that you're the only
one who's responsible for things going right in your life,
you also realize that we all make the same mistakes …
and then you have no choice but to have compassion for
other people. I don't mean compassion like pity, I mean
the ability to put yourself in someone else's shoes and
try to understand why they do what they do.

"When you stop blaming other people for what's going
on, you get your power back."

I didn't understand that until it was too late.

"The love that you don't give today, you will never give.
If you don't tell your loved ones how much you care
about them now, tomorrow may be too late."

It's already too late.

"Be strong."

The door opened and Faith came in.

"I'm really sorry to bother you, but visiting time is
over," she said to my parents.

"Please, miss, just a little longer?" pleaded my mother.

"I'm sorry, the rules are pretty strict about that."

"Come on, sweetheart, we'll come back tomorrow,"
my father said as he helped her up, and then they

moved toward the door.

"Miss, excuse me … How long will it be before he wakes up?" asked my mother.

"I'm afraid we've done everything we can. Now it just depends on fate. He may come around tomorrow, or he may never come around."

That news hit my mom like a slap in the face.

Dad hugged her close and helped her out of the room. Her legs barely held her up. The door closed behind them.

Faith turned to me and said,

"Poor things! Life's so full of hardships, and we have no choice but to deal with them. I guess it may have seemed cruel to tell them what I said, but it would have been even worse to give them false hope."

I guess you're right, I said in my head.

This time she was quiet. She changed my drip, sat by me for a few minutes, and then left the room without saying good-bye.

Please, God, help my parents. I don't care about myself anymore. Do what you like with me, but please, give them the strength to go on.

CHAPTER V

OVER THE NEXT FEW DAYS I REALIZED THAT MY GUIDE WAS RIGHT ABOUT FREEDOM. WE REALLY ARE FREE, BUT THAT MEANS WE'RE FREE TO MAKE MISTAKES. AND WE DO HAVE TO FACE THE CONSEQUENCES OF OUR ACTIONS.

Because we are free, we also create our own futures with every decision we make. Fate doesn't exist. We create our future every waking moment of the day.

Despite the fact that my brother and sisters and I had had the same upbringing, our fates have been very different.

Arthur, two years older than me, was always a successful student. Instead of rebelling like me, he decided, I guess, to take what good he could and put it to work in his life. He's a partner in an architectural firm and has a bright future.

Lorraine, a year younger than me, got married a few months ago. My father didn't like her fiancé; he actually told Lorraine that if she married him she could forget she was his daughter. She stood her ground and she and dad hadn't seen each other since.

Finally there's Grace, everyone's favorite. She's only eight now. When we found out mom was pregnant again, it was a surprise to all of us. When she was born I was delighted. I absolutely adore her, and she loves me very much too.

Bit by bit, my parents began to accept the situation and so did I.

In the following months, I saw aspects of my family that I hadn't seen before: the loving, tender side of my father, my mother's great strength, the cohesion I had never perceived between my brother and sisters.

I suppose that seeing me utterly defenseless and unable to move made them reflect on the fragility of life and face their own vulnerability.

One day Lorraine, her husband, and my father ran into each other in my room. There was no need for words, for explanations or apologies. Lorraine ran to hug my father, and he took her in his arms as if to say,

"I've missed you so much." Then he turned to her husband and said, "Thanks for coming, son" and shook his hand.

That's how he let them know that he had made his peace with their decision and that it had become more important to him to be able to see his daughter than to be self-righteous.

It was a terrible thing that a tragedy had to happen to bring my family together and make them express their love for each other, burying old resentments and disagreements. Why was that? If we were really all so free, why hadn't we chosen to be nice to ourselves and the people around us?

"What we believe." My guide was back to teach me another lesson.

What we believe? I don't understand, I replied.

"Our beliefs determine our existence. Anything you believe about yourself is true. Anything you believe about someone else or about things happening around you is also true—at least it is for you."

I don't get it.

"OK, look: everything you see, feel, hear, or experience is true for you, but not necessarily for anyone else. You experience the things that happen to you in a different way than others do. We each have a unique and distinct way of seeing life."

That's why arguments almost never end in an agreement.

"Exactly! Arguing is a way of trying to make someone else see life as you see it … it's impossible!

"Millions of people die in wars," he went on, "because their leaders want to impose their way of seeing life on other people. All you need is for the president of one country to want to impose on another country his belief that his economic system is better than theirs, or that everybody ought to worship his God, for him to have people killed who don't believe the same."

Millions dead from war—unbelievable! I thought.

"Take Hitler, a madman. He managed to persuade an entire nation that they belonged to a superior race. And six million innocent people suffered the worst kind of atrocities."

But what does this have to do with being nice to people? I asked.

"Everything! What's the thing you most miss right now?"

My health, the ability to move, to express my ideas and feelings. The chance to spend time with the people I love.

"So … you miss the things that you already had."

Yes! It all just came so naturally before, I guess I took my body for granted and I never thought about what a blessing it was.

"Most people waste their time running after superficial stuff, because they think that there's 'something' out there that would make them happy if they had it. They take life's most valuable gifts for granted."

Yeah, we forget about the really important things: our relationships, the things we already have. We always want more and more.

"Humans labor under the misconception that they must have that 'something' to be happy. They don't realize that they already have everything they could possibly need. They don't realize that happiness is just a way of looking at life—a state of mind, a habit."

My life was full of blessings but I was always dissatisfied, I replied.

"Most people fall into that stupid trap of accumulating more and more stuff. Some accumulate wealth and possessions, others knowledge and titles. They're petrified of being poor, of what people will say about them, of not being a worthwhile person. They fail to realize that it's not what they own that makes them worthy, but who they are."

I remember always wanting to be better than other people, to have a better car, be more handsome. Right now I'd give all that away in a heartbeat just to be able to hug my parents.

"We forget that we won't take anything with us when we go, and that all our achievements are worthless if we don't have someone to share them with. Do you see how we act on these erroneous beliefs?"

I thought for a while, then said:

I think you're absolutely right. We're always trying to get more, do more, achieve more, be more. We don't realize that if we stopped a little to enjoy what we already have and be grateful for what we've already achieved or who we already

are, we'd be happy right now. Why is that? Why do almost all
of us do the same? Why do we forget that our relationships
are the most important things in our lives? Why the urge to
ignore what we have and concentrate on what we don't have?

"Because we share a mistaken set of values."

All of us? How is that possible?

"It's possible because we live in a neurotic society that
fosters mistaken beliefs, promotes false values, and
has its priorities all wrong."

It seems hard to believe that we're ALL wrong.

"Really? So how do you explain war? Sending our own
sons and brothers to their deaths to defend our ideas.
How do you explain that the world's wealth is
controlled by ten percent of the population and
everyone else is starving? How do you explain the fact
that people kill for money, that parents pay more
attention to their jobs than to their children and their
families? How do you explain that we're polluting and
destroying our own planet, which is the only place we
have to live, and we're wiping out everything that lives
on it? Tell me, why is it that we watch children starve
to death and do absolutely nothing about it?"

Okay, okay, I think I got it ... Don't get mad.

"I am so over emotions like anger. All I want you to
understand is that the reality of this world has been
created by people and their beliefs. Believing that

there's not enough to go around has caused us to create a reality where poverty exists. Believing that money and power will make us happy has caused us to distance ourselves from our brothers. Thinking that our well-being depends on what happens around us has caused us to lose control of our lives."

You mean our beliefs determine our reality?

"Mind is the forerunner of all things. Whatever you believe will manifest in your life."

So if I believe I can walk again, laugh, run, hug, cry …?

I heard someone arguing outside the door to my room and recognized Faith's voice saying,

"You can't go in there, miss. A family member must be present."

"I don't want to see his family, I want to see him," said a woman who for a moment I didn't recognize.

"Besides, doesn't this make me family?" she added cryptically.

"Are you his girlfriend?" asked Faith.

"Mind your own damn business! Let me in!"

The door was flung open and there she was. Finally, Laura had come to visit me.

She walked closer to the bed, with Faith trying to stop her. As soon as she saw me she went so pale I thought she was going to faint. When Faith saw the expression on her face, she stopped trying to prevent her from seeing me and laid a hand on her shoulder to comfort her.

Laura just stood there motionless, looking at me as if I were a ghost. Then after a few moments she started screaming, "You bastard! How could you do this to yourself? How could you do this to me?" Tears poured down her face. "What am I supposed to do now? Look at me!" She touched her stomach and it was obvious she was seven or eight months pregnant.

I mentally flinched as she flung herself at the bed trying to scratch my face. Unfortunately, Faith grabbed her arms and held her back. I say unfortunately because at that moment I understood perfectly how furious she was and would happily have let her hurt me to vent her anger. I would have done anything to lessen the guilt I felt. I would have done anything to have her touch me.

Faith had a firm grip on Laura's arms as she struggled to get free.

"Let go of me, damn you! Let me go!" She thrashed about like a madwoman.

"Try to calm down. You're going to hurt yourself. You won't do yourself any good," Faith kept telling her.

Slowly she began to settle down. She stopped struggling and let Faith hold her. By then there were two hospital security guards in the room, tall guys in white uniforms. Faith gestured to them that she had everything under control and didn't need them. When the men left, Laura and Faith followed them out of the room.

My mind was a whirlwind of conflicting sentiments. On one hand I was glad to know that Laura was alive. On the other I was devastated to see her suffering so much. And … she was pregnant! God, why now, when I couldn't do a thing for them? What would happen to her and the baby? Why was this happening to me?

"Oh woe is me! Why is this happening to me?" my guide mimicked mockingly. "Things don't happen to YOU … mind is the forerunner of all things."
Fuck you! Fuck you and your fucking cryptic wisdom bringing it to me now! I felt about to explode with rage and had a sharp pain in my chest.
"Ignorance, arrogance, suffering …"

That was the last thing I heard before something strange happened …

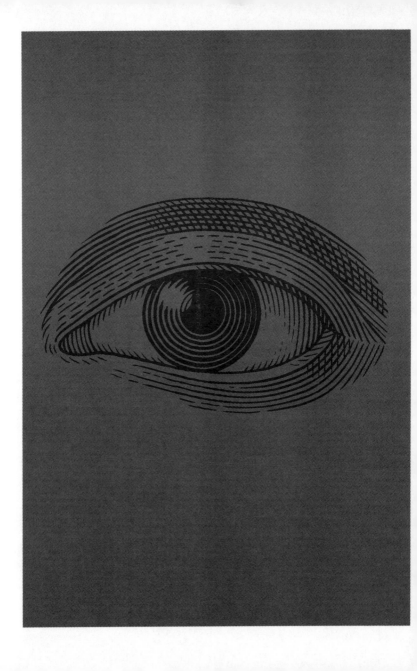

CHAPTER VI

FOR A FEW MOMENTS, MY FIELD OF VISION CHANGED COMPLETELY. I WAS NO LONGER LOOKING AT THE SHABBY LAMP ON THE CEILING, I WAS LOOKING DOWN … AT MYSELF! I SAW MY IMMOBILE BODY, WEAK AND WASTED; I SAW MY HAGGARD FACE WITH THE EYES WIDE OPEN AND AN AWFUL AGONIZED EXPRESSION. I FINALLY UNDERSTOOD WHY EVERYONE WAS TERRIFIED TO LOOK AT ME.

Everything passed before my eyes in slow motion. I could hear an alarm on the machine by the bed warning that my heart had stopped beating. I saw doctors and several nurses, Faith among them, run into the room. I saw them hastily check cables and flip switches.

A feeling of immense tranquility and total indifference washed over me. In a matter of a few seconds I remembered all the most important things that had happened in my life. Actually, I didn't just remember them, I relived them.

I relived the warmth and safety of my mother's embrace when I was a baby. I smelled her perfume and saw the tenderness in her eyes, felt her affection and her love for me.

I relived happy moments with people I loved. I heard the

laughter and felt the joy of sharing my life with them.

In seconds I ran through all the moments that had been special for me: the first time I saw the sea, the warmth of the sun on my skin, my first kiss, the flavor of my favorite food, all the beautiful landscapes I'd seen, my favorite tune, being with Laura …

I wish I could be with Laura again and get to know the baby.

That was the last thing that entered my mind in those marvelous moments. What happened next was not so pleasant … a strong electric shock brought me back inside my body. I could see a doctor leaning over me holding two paddles to my chest. Another electric shock made my back arch and sent a spasm through my body.

"We got a pulse," yelled someone in the background.
"Vitals are back," said one of the nurses.

Everyone began to move away but the doctor, who was still standing over me looked at me with a brooding expression.

"What is it?" asked Faith.
"I just don't know if I'm doing the right thing by keeping him alive," he answered.
"It's the right thing. It's your job," said Faith, patting

him twice on the back.

"I don't think he'll last long anyway," he said coldly.

The doctor checked that the machines around the bed were working correctly, then left, asking Faith to call my parents and let them know what had happened.

Despite the pain and discomfort of being back in my body, I still felt the peace that had washed over me moments before. I also had a mental clarity that until then I had never experienced. It was as if suddenly all my worries, fears, and insecurities had disappeared. As if I had suddenly recovered a deep wisdom that had been lost. I felt as if, for a few seconds, I had been granted a wider perspective. Had been all things, strangely, all at once: the doctors, the nurses, the sunlight, the walls, the birds chirping outside. As if the bubble of consciousness that is "me" had popped. It was back now— "I" was back—but something had changed in me ... I had changed.

I didn't understand what just happened. Maybe my brain was still getting enough oxygen to keep me alive and I had imagined everything, or maybe I had reached a higher plane of consciousness.

It doesn't really matter. My one certainty was that my desire to be with Laura and see the baby was keeping me alive. I was a mix of stories, memories, expectations, beliefs, preferences, experiences, aspirations, desires ... all of them unique and all of them unrepeatable. Being with each other, being with others, loving others, was so important. I knew more than ever that this was what I wanted and needed above all other things: love and connection with others. Love and connection with others. It was so beautiful just to feel that knowing. To be so clear. Finally.

I suddenly found I didn't mind my condition so much; the joy of being here and of being able to participate in life, even just as a spectator, was well worth it.

"Nothing like a little taste of death to make you appreciate life," I heard my guide say. "You still mad at me?"

Oh, I'm SO over emotions like anger, I teased.

"Ha! Death put you in a good mood!"

A miracle just happened to me.

"Life is a miracle, you're right. Most people forget that. They focus on the problems, on what's missing, on pointless endeavors, on stupid preoccupations. People get used to waking up each morning, to feeling their heartbeat, to the wonder of their senses; they get used to the possibility of expressing their ideas, their love, their individuality, and they forget that each of those gifts is a miracle in itself. They take the gift of life, and waste it."

It's such a tragedy, I said.

"Death's your advisor. Your best friend. I don't mean

you should get obsessed with it or wish yourself dead or get depressed because it's inevitable, but just remember that the days are numbered for all of us. We can just cease to exist at any time. Keeping that in mind puts everything in perspective. When death makes an appearance, the little problems of daily life don't seem so serious any more, worrying seems pointless; the arguments, the hate, and the resentment disappear from our relationships because we want to make the most of the time we have left."

It feels as if what happened made me wake up.

"You had to die to live. Our conversations are going to be a lot more interesting from now on."

I've always been asleep.

"Most people live in a dream their entire lives, and the worst thing is that it's not even a nice dream. They can't see beyond what they've been told they have to do. They're dragged along by a routine that they have no idea how to get out of. They're trapped in ways of behaving that don't deliver the results they want, in argumentative relationships that don't satisfy them, in searches for things that don't belong to them, in habits they detest."

As if they were robots programmed to work, be productive, and acquire what other people tell them they need. They just react automatically to what they've been made to believe.

They've never learned to think for themselves! To see the truth! To live!

"Blindly following beliefs imposed on them, unquestioned beliefs passed down from generation to generation."

But how can you break free from something you've believed your whole life? The habits, the patterns, the routines are so deep.

"Mind is the forerunner of all things."

I wish I could share this with the whole world. Run to the highest mountain and shout it out loud!

"What would you tell them?"

I'd tell them to question their beliefs. I'd encourage them to rethink how they think. I'd tell them "mind is the forerunner of all things" and that what matters isn't what happens to you but, rather, how you react to what happens.

My guide laughed a joyous laugh.

"You're getting it! A person who wants to wake up and stop being a slave to his upbringing, society, and the past must put everything he believes to the test. It's the only way to be free again. Luckily, you and I still have the opportunity to do this."

I thought of my condition and felt a wave of despair. But then

I remembered that I get to choose how to respond to everything and I felt better, felt lighter and happier and more optimistic about my life—even as it was.

Yeah, that's great, I said.

CHAPTER VII

THAT SAME NIGHT MY FATHER CAME TO VISIT ME
WITH ARTHUR AND LORRAINE. FAITH HAD CALLED
THEM ABOUT MY HEART STOPPING AND MY BEING
BROUGHT BACK TO LIFE. LORRAINE CAME TO
THE BED WHILE MY FATHER AND ARTHUR SPOKE
QUIETLY BY THE DOOR. I COULDN'T HEAR WHAT
THEY WERE SAYING.

"My poor brother," Lorraine whispered, crying and
holding my hand.
*Hi, Lorraine. It's nice to see you again. I'm fine, don't worry.
Really. Better than ever,* I imagined myself saying.

Lorraine had always been good to me. We never were very open
about our feelings with one another, but we both knew we
could rely on each other when we needed to, and that feeling
went beyond words.

The doctor knocked twice before he opened the door and
asked if he could have a moment alone with my father. Lorraine
and Arthur left the room and the doctor pulled a couple of
chairs up next to the bed so he and my father could talk.

"How's my son doing, doctor?" my father asked anxiously.

"Not very well, I'm afraid. His condition has been deteriorating lately. His heart stopped beating today, and although his vital signs are stable right now there's a good possibility it might happen again."

"Is he going to die soon?"

"We can't know for certain. It's been eight months already and this is the first time it's happened. But his heart could stop at any time and we might be unable to bring him back. That's why I wanted to talk with you in private … I need you to sign some forms," he said, taking several sheets of paper out of a folder and handing them to my father.

My father began to read. Suddenly he leapt to his feet, started crumpling the sheets of paper between his hands, and throwing them at the doctor yelling, "Are you crazy? You want me to sign an order to let my own son die?"

The doctor, taken aback, stood up and knocked over his chair. He put one hand out to steady himself on the wall and another up to protect his face from the flying balls of paper.

"Calm down, sir! That's not what this is about," he said.

Arthur had heard my father yelling and, knowing

what his temper was like, rushed in to see what was going on.

"What's the matter, Dad?" he asked, positioning himself between my father and the doctor to defuse the situation.

"I'm not giving up on my son! I'm not!"

"Okay, okay, but what's going on?" said Arthur, looking from my father to the doctor to try to understand.

"We need an authorization not to resuscitate him the next time his heart stops beating," explained the doctor as he picked up the crumpled pieces of paper from the floor. "It's what is best," he said, handing the forms to my brother and walking out visibly rattled.

"What is best! What does he know?" my father said.

"Dad, he's the doctor that saved your son this afternoon …"

"And now he wants to kill him," snapped my father angrily.

Arthur read the forms that doctor had given him carefully, then sighed deeply and said, "Dad, you have to understand … it's been eight months … eight months of stress for all of us. Mom doesn't even know what happened today. Besides, how much have you spent on this hospital?"

"Money? Money doesn't matter! Money is the last thing we should be thinking about!" shouted my father

and clenching his fists. A second later he realized that
he was back to his old behavior and, abashed, he
apologized:

"I'm sorry, son, I'm at my wits' end."

"I know, Dad, this is hard on all of us."

My dad cried.

"What'll happen to your mother when she finds out?"

"Mom has gotten a lot stronger with this whole
experience. Dad, it's been so long now, don't you
think she's coming around to the idea?"

"You can never come round to the idea of losing a
child," my father answered. "You don't know pain until
you've lost a child."

"I mean she knows it's only a question of time. Look,"
my brother pointed at me, "if he ever does wake up,
will he ever be normal again? He's been like this for so
long … we don't even know if his brain is still
working."

Better than you could ever imagine! I answered inside my
head. *I'm great!*

"But it's not up to us to decide that," said my father,
taking Arthur's hand in his to stop him from pointing
at me. "That's playing God."

"Keeping him alive is playing God! Maybe God was
the one that stopped his heart and keeping him here is
against God's will. Maybe he's suffering and all we're

doing is drawing it out."

My father dropped into a chair and wept, covering his face with his hands, murmuring "Damn it ... Damn it ... Damn it ... It's like a cruel fucking joke. Fuck you, God! Fuck you! You hear me, you fucking son of a bitch!"

Dad's sobbing filled the room. I was touched by the depth of his love for me that he would take on God. "Sign the authorization, Dad," Arthur said after my father's storm of sorrow passed. He handed dad the bunch of crumpled forms.

My father stared at them for a few moments, then mechanically reached into his jacket for his pen, wiped a tear from his face, and signed my death sentence.

"Don't be so melodramatic!" My guide wasn't one to keep his opinion to himself. "We're all going to die. The important thing isn't to live for a long time but to make the most of the time we're alive."

It seems strange that I'm not angry with my dad or my brother, I thought to him.

"Forgiving is not an action in itself; forgiving is simply understanding. When you realize that we're all trying to do what we think is best, that our actions are usually well-intentioned, that everything we do is aimed at bringing us closer to what we believe is happiness, then you realize there's nothing to forgive."

What about when someone hurts you deliberately?

"They probably were hurt when they were young, of course. And you can only feel compassion, can't you?"

I get it.

"We all do our best. We have all been given different information."

There's so much bad information out there.

After a while, Lorraine came into the room. After my father and brother explained to her what had happened, they all thought it a good idea to tell my mother so she could prepare herself mentally. Lorraine and my father went home and Arthur agreed to drop the forms off at the doctor's office.

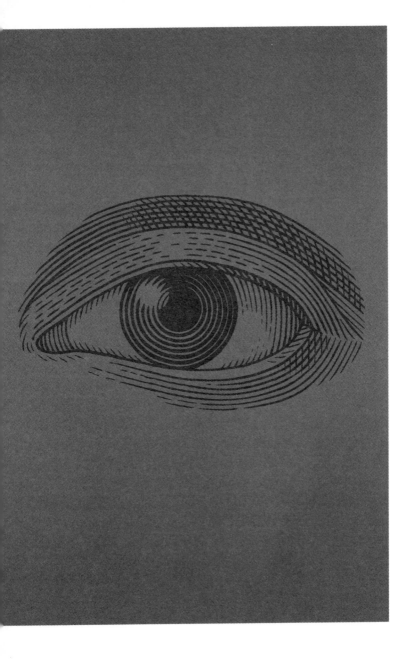

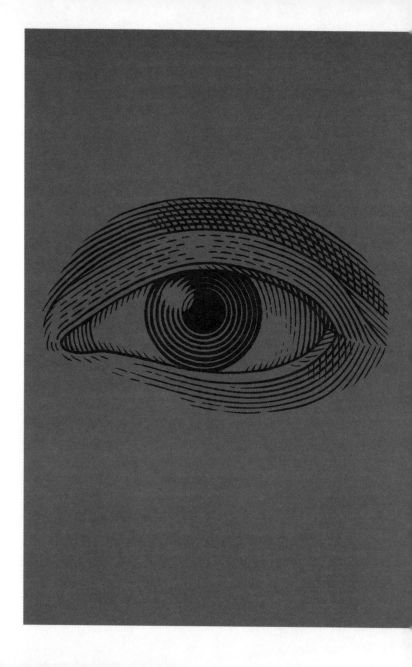

CHAPTER VIII

THE NEXT DAY LAURA CAME TO VISIT ME AGAIN AND FOUND MY PARENTS IN THE ROOM. THEY HADN'T SEEN EACH OTHER SINCE THE DAY OF THE ACCIDENT AND THEY DIDN'T KNOW SHE WAS PREGNANT. SHE SEEMED CALMER. HER RAGE FROM THE PREVIOUS DAY HAD MELLOWED INTO A PROFOUND SADNESS.

She explained to them what had happened the night of the accident:

"We had a big fight at the party," she told my mother. "He'd had a lot to drink and was in a bad way. He walked off with his friend Edward and when they came back the two of them were acting really crazy. They were all glassy-eyed and saying stuff that didn't make sense. They'd already decided to leave the party. I tried to stop them but I couldn't. They could hardly stand, but they got into Edward's car and drove off with the tires squealing. I just stood there and watched them drive away. When they got to the corner they ran a red light …"

She paused and stared down at the floor, trying to remember exactly what she had seen. My mother put her hand to her mouth as if to stifle a sob; my father put his arm around her, and Laura continued:

"There was this tractor-trailer truck … it crashed right into the driver's side of the car. I don't think the guy even had time to brake. He hit them so hard the car flipped over a few times then landed upside down. I ran over to the car and when I saw them there, all mangled up with bits of metal and glass, covered in blood, I was sure they were both dead."

"What happened then? What did you do? Where did you go?" asked my father.

"I don't really remember. I remember people crowding around the car and pushing past me to see what had happened. I started to walk away … like I was sleepwalking. I just kept going. I had no idea where I was. I don't remember how I got home."

"But why didn't you call us?" asked my mother. "We were so worried about you. We don't have your address or phone number."

"I'm really sorry. I was so afraid. After what happened I got really depressed and went to stay for a while with an aunt who lives a long way away. I was trying to get over the whole thing, because I thought they were dead."

"And the baby? Is it ..."

"It's his, it's your son's child," she interrupted my mother.

"He never said a thing."

"He didn't know. I was going to tell him at the party, but I never got the chance."

"You poor thing!" said my mother. She hugged Laura and began to cry.

Laura hugged her back and glanced over at my father to see how he would react. He hugged them both tightly in support. They stayed like that for a few moments, then Laura said, "I came to town for a check-up and found out he was here. That's how I found him," she said, her eyes welling up with tears.

"Be strong, honey," my mother said, taking her hand and turning to look at me too.

They continued to talk about what had happened and about the pregnancy. I learned that Laura's due date was in just three weeks. I was surprised by how calm everyone seemed, and I understood why my guide had said I was ignorant for complaining about my situation.

"We all have an inner strength that brings us though the worst possible situations," said my guide. "Time and time again, we get over the pain of losing the things we love."

Although at the time we feel like the world is ending and we'll never be strong enough to stand the pain, I answered. "It's at times like these that we have to try to remember we've already made it through difficult situations. We have to make an effort to understand that it hurts so bad because we're sensitive, loving beings. If we didn't care about anything we wouldn't feel the pain, but we'd also lose the biggest joy there is: loving other people."

If you think about it, I interrupted, *loving other people is an act of bravery. We love despite knowing we will inevitably lose whom or what we love, despite knowing that it could all end, and that we have no guarantee of getting anything in return.*

"You don't need to get anything in exchange for love you give, because loving other people is a gift you give yourself."

So why is love always attended by so much suffering?

"Because what most people call love, isn't. What makes you suffer is egotism and arrogance."

Explain that for me, please?

"People who say they suffer for love are really suffering because they believe that the person they love should do as they wish—and that's arrogance.

A person who suffers because he thinks his beloved should satisfy his needs is selfish.

"What most people call love is more like a business contract that says, 'I agree to love you provided that you are what I want you to be and provided that you do what I say.' The truth is that love is free; it makes no demands, it doesn't want to change the other person, it isn't possessive, it isn't conditional."

It's paradoxical that we're so strong and yet we suffer so much.

"Many people are used to suffering and being unhappy. They're so used to it that they make unhappiness part of their identity and personality; that's why they have such a hard time being happy. They focus on the negative things and forget about the blessings they receive every day."

So, what, we're not supposed to be hurt by anything? I asked.

"Pain is not the same as suffering. Pain is part of life and it comes from losing something we love. Suffering comes from refusing to accept what's happening, from the idea that things could be different, from thinking that things should go the way YOU want them to."

So are we responsible for our lives or not? You first tell me that we have the power to make what we want of our lives, and then you say we should just accept what happens.

"You're responsible for YOUR life, not life itself.
Here's another paradox: you have absolutely no
power, and yet you have all the power."

*It's like my situation right now: I can't do anything to
change what's happening, I have no power over that; but as
soon as I accept this, which I do have power over, I stop
suffering. What seemed to me like a punishment just a few
days ago now looks more like a blessing, an opportunity
to spend a few more moments with the people I love and
to be part of their lives. Just a few days ago I wanted to
die, and now all I want is to last another three weeks so
I can see my baby.*

"Nothing out there has changed, just your attitude
about what's happening. That's the greatest power
that humans have: the capacity to decide how to
react to what life throws at them. You can't control
what happens around you, but you can decide
how to interpret it and what attitude to take. You're
responsible for what you think, for the decisions you
make, for how you want to see and experience life."

I'm also responsible for myself and no one else.

"Exactly. The one thing that can fill your life with the
most suffering and frustration is believing that you're
responsible for what other people feel, think, or do. A
lot of people take on the guilt, pain, and suffering of
others as if, by doing that, they're helping them in

some way. Believing that someone depends on you to be happy, besides being supremely arrogant, is a useless burden that's too heavy for anyone to carry. Everyone is responsible for his or her own life."

I was so engrossed in this inner conversation that I didn't realize my parents had left the room, leaving Laura alone with me. She pulled a chair up to the bed, took my hand in hers and began to cry silently as she gazed into my face. Then she looked over at the door, as if to make sure it was closed, leaned over secretively and whispered,

"Hi, sweetheart. I really miss you …"

She choked up and had to stop speaking. She laid her arm across my chest and her head on the pillow next to mine. I felt her tears running down my face and her scent brought back memories of times we spent together.

I wanted more than anything to stroke her hair, dry her tears with kisses, and tell her that I missed her too, that it was because of her I was still here. I wanted to tell her how much I love her and ask her to forgive me for the bad times I had put her through.

She stayed like that for a few more seconds, then lifted her head to look at me. I was surprised to see her crying and smiling at the same time, showing the strength of character that my guide and I had been talking about.

"How about that big, fat old belly," she said jokingly, stroking her stomach. "It's your baby. He's going to be born soon." She was pensive for a moment, then went on. "This baby is a product of our love. I know our relationship wasn't perfect, but I always knew that you loved me."

As she talked she kept veering wildly between laughter and tears, in a strange mix of joy and sadness.

I love you so much. If I treated you badly it's because I was under a misconception, I imagined myself saying. *Thanks for being here for me, despite everything.*

"Honey, what's going to happen to us?" she said with a sigh.

Whatever happens, it'll all be alright, you'll see,
I answered, safe in the knowledge that we have the strength to face up to all of life's challenges, no matter how difficult they are.

Even the final and greatest challenge.

CHAPTER IX

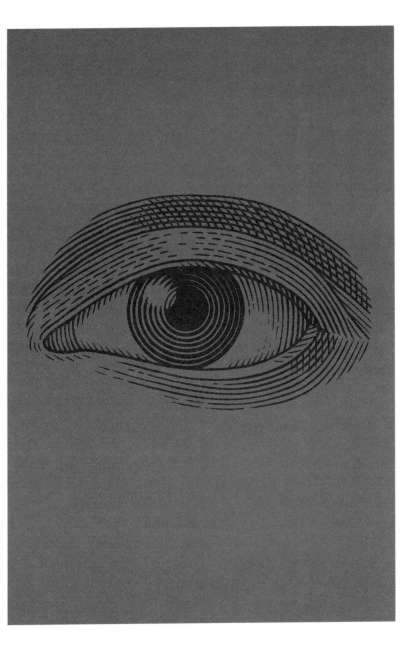

THE NEXT TWO WEEKS PASSED UNEVENTFULLY. I KEPT HAVING CONVERSATIONS IN MY MIND WITH MY GUIDE, AND LEARNED MORE FROM THEM THAN I HAD IN MY ENTIRE LIFE ABOUT TRUE HUMAN VALUES, ABOUT OUR ABILITIES, ABOUT RESPONSIBILITY. AND ABOUT A THOUSAND OTHER MATTERS.

The hospital made some changes to visiting hours and let someone from my family stay with me and sleep in my room; after all, my heart was likely to stop beating at any moment. They set up a cot by the wall so my mother could spend the night next to me. Sometimes my father or brother or sister stayed instead, to give her a break. My mother always protested, saying she wanted to be there just in case. They would convince her by saying that whoever was staying with me would call her immediately if anything happened.

One night I was mildly surprised to see that no one had come to stay. I didn't think too much of it because I supposed that someone from the family would turn up at some point.

It was probably about eleven that night when the door suddenly opened and the nurse that used to look after me before Faith arrived—the stony-faced, bad-tempered one—

appeared with a doctor I hadn't seen before. They both looked around shiftily to make sure no one was seeing them, then came in and shut the door. The nurse pointed at the bed without looking at me, and said:

"That's the one I was telling you about."

The doctor came over to get a look. He thought for a moment, then asked:

"How long did you say he's been in a coma?"
"About eight and a half months. I think he's perfect for what we need," she replied.
"How do you know his organs are in good condition?" the doctor asked.
"About two weeks ago he was declared clinically dead for six minutes and they managed to revive him. Since then his vitals have been stable. It's all working just fine," replied the obnoxious nurse.

The doctor still seemed to have misgivings. He kept rubbing his chin and looking toward the door as if he were afraid someone might walk in at any moment and find him there.

"It's too risky," he finally said. "To begin with, there's the alarm on the machine, and what if his family shows up? I'm not sure it's worth it."

"Of course it's worth it!" the nurse interrupted. "They'll give us five thousand dollars for each of his kidneys. His old man already signed the do-not-resuscitate order if he has a cardiac arrest. I'll take care of the alarm—I can disconnect it. And you don't need to worry about his family: I know they're not coming in today."

"Did you check that the blood type matches?" he asked.

"They're both O positive."

"Any history of disease?" insisted the doctor, trying to find a reason that would persuade her not to go ahead.

"He's clean."

"How are we going to get him straight down to the morgue?"

"I'm in charge of recording entries into the morgue. It's not a problem."

"And how do we explain that we were here when it happened?"

"Look, I've just been reassigned to take care of this patient. No one will give it a second thought. And you're on duty tonight, aren't you? What's to be suspicious of? I'm doing my rounds, I found him dead and called you in to certify it."

"I don't know … I have a bad feeling about this," said

the doctor, scratching his head and looking at
me again.

"Don't think about it anymore. If you're not doing it
for the money, think of the woman who's going to get
his kidneys. She has her whole life ahead of her. She
has two kids waiting for her at home. He, on the other
hand, isn't going anywhere. His body's alive but his
brain is dead. Look at him."

The doctor glanced at me and then lowered his gaze as if he
sensed that I was aware of what was going on, and looked like
he felt ashamed.

"Okay," he said, letting out a sigh. "Switch off the
alarm. I'll make sure no one comes close."

The nurse began to move some of the cables on the back of the
machine that was keeping me alive. As she did this, the doctor
opened the door a crack and peeked out, visibly nervous.

"Done!" she said, standing back and rubbing her hands
on her uniform like a child caught touching something
she shouldn't.

The doctor took one last glance outside the room, then closed
the door silently and moved over to the machine.

"Pay attention," he said. "You see these seven switches? You have to turn them off one by one at hourly intervals to avoid any abrupt changes. That's the only way to keep the organs in good condition so we can use them. It's twelve o'clock," he said looking at his watch. "Turn off the first one and come back in an hour."

The nurse moved over to the control panel and flipped the first switch. I felt my heart rate drop and suddenly felt drowsy, as if I were about to fall asleep.

"You have to switch the others off in this order," he said, pointing to the switches from left to right and mopping sweat from his brow with the sleeve of his white coat. "You take care of this and I'll make the preparations for the transplant. If anything goes wrong, we're going to be in a lot of trouble."
"You worry too much," was the last thing the nurse said to him as they both hurried out of the room.

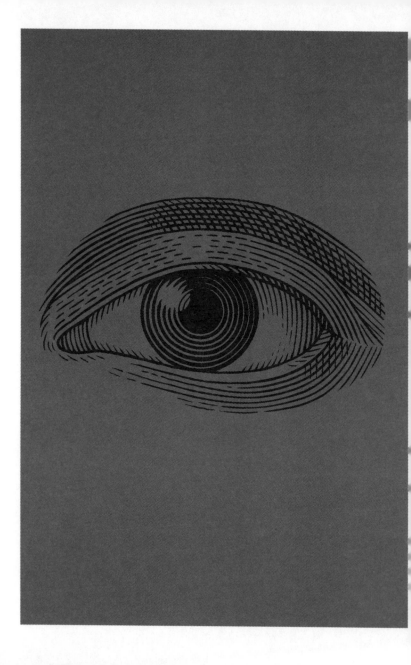

CHAPTER X

A FEW MINUTES AFTER THE DOCTOR AND THE NURSE
LEFT, FAITH CAME INTO THE ROOM AND I BEGAN TO
THINK I MIGHT HAVE A CHANCE TO STAY ALIVE.
I DIDN'T WANT TO DIE, NOT YET. I WANTED TO SEE
MY BABY.

She sat next to me on the bed, looked at me tenderly for a
moment, stroked my hair like she always did and said,

"Hi there. I came to say good-bye."
Good-bye! Do you have any idea what's going on? I yelled
to her inside my head.
"My work here with you is done."
Wait, please don't go. I answered. *Look at the control
panel! Put the switch back up!*
"By the way ..." she smiled and hesitated over what
she was about to say, then continued, "Laura went into
labor tonight at about ten o'clock. They expect the
baby to be born in about six hours. Your whole family
is with her right now, that's why no one came to see
you this evening."
All the more reason to flip the switch! Flip the switch! Flip

the switch! I screamed in my mind, trying as hard as I could to invoke telepathic powers.

"There's nothing I can do for you now. I have to go where someone else needs me. I hope I was of some use to you."

It was a huge help, Faith," I said resignedly. *Thanks to you and the care you gave me I managed to make it through the first few months in this place. You taught me what it is to love unconditionally and to be dedicated to looking after other people without expecting anything in return. Thank you so much.*

"I wish I could have done more, but …" she fell silent for a few moments, hung her head and, wiping away a tear that ran down her cheek, went on, "It'll all be okay, you'll see. It's time for me to leave." She kissed me on the forehead and left the room without looking back.

Good-bye, Faith. God bless you. Thanks for everything. Thank you for being you.

So finally the uncertainty was over. I had another six hours to live and I would never get to meet my child. I consciously tried to feel angry at the two people who were ruining my plans, but I couldn't. Despite the fact that they were motivated at least in part by greed, the result, if they managed to use my kidneys to save the woman they had spoken about, would be positive.

This could be my last good deed, and although I would not have played an active role in it, I would contribute part of my body so that someone else could continue to enjoy this marvelous life.

How ironic! In another part of this hospital my baby was waiting his turn to begin living and I was here waiting my turn to die, as if there were some kind of special connection between him and me.

"There IS a special connection between your baby and you!" said my guide. "And not just between you two, but with all of humanity, all living things and everything that exists."

Sure, we're all part of the universe.

"You aren't part of the universe, you ARE the universe. You're life itself."

I'm life itself? That sounds deep, I remarked. *I don't think the six hours I have left is enough time for you to explain that to me.*

"I'm not going to explain. Under the circumstances, I'm going to cheat and show you something that few humans experience in their entire lifetimes. Pass out …"

What? How am I supposed to just …?

I hadn't even finished the question when I realized I was no longer in the hospital room, or inside my body. It was like one of those dreams where anything is possible, where you realize that you're dreaming and you know what's happening without needing to see it or hear it.

"This is enlightenment," said my guide. "This is what wise men seek and gurus and teachers wish to attain. This is what years and years of profound meditation get you."

What is this place? Heaven?

"It's not a place, it's a feeling. There is no time or space here in the way that you knew them before."

But …

"Shhh! Switch off your thoughts and let yourself feel …"

I let myself go completely, and in a matter of seconds I understood what a great gift my guide had given me: "Enlightenment," as he called it, is an amazing feeling of being part of the universe and at the same time being the universe. You feel a connection with all of humankind, all living beings, and everything that exists. It was just like when the bubble of my consciousness had popped when I died before, only it was ongoing and ongoing and ongoing—a timeless peaceful amazing bliss of the most incredible warmth and love. I had no fear of being alone and realized that life looks after us, just as it looks after everything that exists … that everything is right and that we are all a part of something much bigger … a beautiful and complex design made from love. There were questions but I didn't feel any need for answers. Even this "not knowing" was just fine. Just fine.

✳

"It's time for you to come back."

My guide's voice was the slightest whisper, insisting that I wake up from this beautiful dream.

Once again I felt that I was in my body, and despite a terrible weariness I still felt the sensation of well-being that the experience had given.

✳

That was amazing! I thought excitedly. *I'm part of everything that exists! I'm as important as the stars, the sun, and everything else in the universe! We are all the same!*
"And that's not just mystical or spiritualistic crap. It's a provable fact," replied my guide and then went on, "You were created from one of your father's cells and one of your mother's cells. Those two cells had all the genetic information from all of your ancestors. You're connected to all of humanity. At the end of the day, we're all related."
But I didn't just feel a connection with humans—it was with everything, I said, intrigued.

"When you were conceived in your mother's womb, her body and your two cells had all the information in them they needed to create every part of your body. There was a perfect plan to form you exactly as you are now. The smallest details were already planned: the color of your eyes, hair, and skin, the shape of your mouth, the dimples in your cheeks, the hair on your body, and exactly where each of them would grow.

"Your mother's body took the raw material to make you from everything surrounding her: the air she was breathing, the water she drank, and the food she ate. You were formed out of parts of the universe.

"An apple that was once part of an animal and before that an insect and way before that the petal of a rose, was used to make your heart. Water that was once a river and before that an iceberg at the North Pole and then a cloud and rain, was used to make the blood that runs through your veins. And minerals that were once a mountain and long, long before that a distant star, were used to make your bones.

"When you die and your body disintegrates, the particles it releases will become raw material that the universe will use to keep renewing itself."

Is that why you say I'm life itself?

"Through you, life is sustained and renewed. You are

the instrument that life has used to create another miraculous being that is full of possibilities: the baby waiting to be born a few feet from here. That new being will come to give something very special to the world, something that only he can give, a wonderful gift for the whole universe."

You mean my baby will be special? That my purpose in life was to bring him into the world?

"He's as special as you and every other human being. The gift he'll give to the world is his own individuality, because despite the fact that he's part of everything that exists, he'll also be unique. That baby will come here to share his thoughts and his ideas, his personality, his emotions, his happiness, and his sadness. That's the purpose of our lives: to give the world the gift of our uniqueness, our individuality."

To be ourselves, that's the meaning of life! I interrupted.

"To be what we are and to enjoy this unique opportunity to exist. Before you were born you were part of eternity, and when you die you'll be part of it again. You've been given a short time to be yourself and you can take advantage of it."

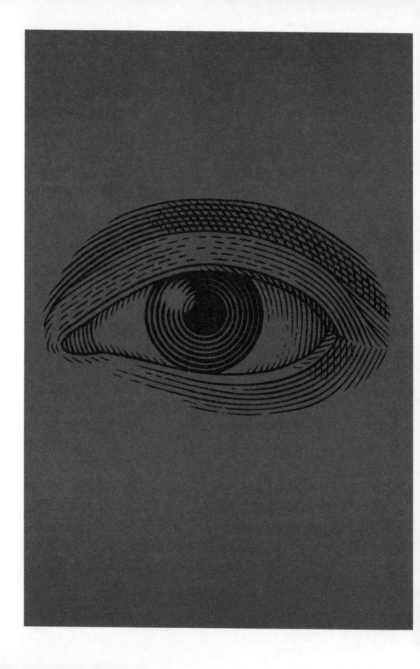

CHAPTER XI

AT THAT POINT, THE DOOR OPENED SUDDENLY AND THE NURSE WHO WAS NOW MY EXECUTIONER ENTERED. SHE CLOSED THE DOOR CAREFULLY SO AS NOT TO MAKE A NOISE, TURNED OFF THE NEXT SWITCH, AND THEN HURRIED OUT, MAKING SURE THAT NO ONE SAW HER.

I panicked slightly when I noticed that my breathing was getting slower. My head started to spin and my sight clouded over for a moment. Slowly my body got used to the decreased supply of oxygen, the dizziness passed, and I just felt weary.

I was no longer afraid or angry, but a great wave of sadness washed over me.

"That sadness comes from guilt and resentment," said my guide. "Make the most of the time you have to forgive others and, most importantly, to forgive yourself."

I immediately realized he was right and began to imagine that I was writing a series of letters to the most important people in my life. I started with my parents.

DEAR MOM & DAD,

I'm writing this at the moment of my death to say good-bye and to thank you for all the blessings you filled my life with.

I now understand that everything you did for me, you did out of love. That despite all the mistakes I made and the bad times I put you through by being ignorant, you were always ready to help me. I realize that you always acted in my best interests and did the best you could.

I now understand that you also have a history of good and bad experiences, that you also have wounds and fears like everyone else, and that you always acted according to what you thought was best for us all.

I want to apologize for blaming you for the things that went wrong in my life, and I admit right here and now that I was the only person responsible for my actions. I was free to choose my fate, and it's my own fault that I'm in the situation I'm in.

I want to apologize for judging you and for focusing on your weaknesses and defects. I now know that I had no right to do that, because nobody knows what it is to be in your shoes, and

I now understand that it's a mistake to want to change people, that we should accept them as they are.

I hope that one day you'll understand that I'm proud to have been your son, and that if I had been given the chance to choose my parents, I would have chosen you.

I'm very sorry for the pain I've caused you. I'm sure that your love for each other will give you the strength to get over this situation and all the other difficult situations that life presents.

Mom, Dad, thank you for loving me and taking care of me. Thank you for being patient with me and teaching me things. Thank you for giving me life.

I love you,

Your son

When I finished writing that imaginary letter, I felt as if a weight I'd been carrying was lifted off me. It had made my progress through life slow and tiresome, yet I had clung to it.

Next I imagined that I was writing a letter to the baby I didn't know.

DEAR SON OR DAUGHTER,

While you are waiting to see light for the first time, the spark of my life is slowly going out.

I'm amazed that even though I haven't set eyes on you one single time, the simple fact that I found out you exist fills the last moments of my life with joy and hope.

I can't explain why it is that despite having never held you in my arms, I'm filled with the deepest love for you. It's probably because for me, and for everyone else, you represent a ray of hope for a better world, or because you're the proof that someone up there still thinks we can make a better job of our lives and that we deserve another chance at happiness.

Please don't let my death become a scar on your life. You must always know that I made my own decisions and that I had to face up to the consequences of my actions. You are a new human being and you don't have to suffer for the mistakes that I have made. Don't let anyone try to make my death into a tragedy, because it's not. We all die sooner or later, and we all leave behind wasted opportunities for things we might have done. But the things we would have done don't exist; only what we do is real.

Don't let the fact that you don't have a father affect you too much. We can all accept reality, as long as we don't cling to what might have been. Because what might have been doesn't exist either; only what is real exists.

Open your heart to receive love from your mother and all those around you. If you do, you'll realize that you don't need my love or my presence. There will still be enough love for you once I'm gone.

Give the world the great gift of your love and your personality. Don't let fear stop you from doing what you want. Trust that you are a miracle and that life wants to care for you as it cares for all its children.

Enjoy your life and make it a wonderful experience.

I love you,

Your dad

Then I started on a letter to Laura.

DEAR LAURA,

Today I realize that I spent a large part of my life living in the future, filling myself with fear over what might happen and imagining what should be. By living like this, I often ruined precious moments we had together.

Most people spend their lives looking to the future, making plans and imagining what will happen and what they want to achieve. From here, on my deathbed, it all looks different. From this perspective, I can see things in my life for what they really were. From here I can see that the important things in life aren't achievements or goals, or amassing wealth or knowledge, or showing the world how much we're worth; the really important thing is to be with our loved ones. The kisses, the hugs, the caresses, the laughs, the sharing, our love for each other: this is what we're meant to spend our time on.

I know I put you through some hard times by trying to change you. I didn't realize that I had no right to, because you didn't belong to me. I hope you understand that my failings weren't motivated by bad will, but ignorance, the fear of being hurt, the mistaken notion *that I didn't deserve your love, and my fear of commitment to you.*

I want to apologize for my mistakes and set you free from my demands and my needs. It was never your responsibility to make up for my deficiencies, and you were never responsible for making me happy.

All I have in my heart is joy that I met you, gratitude for the happy time we spent together, and my love for you.

I love you,

Your beloved

Finally, I began to imagine that I was writing the most important letter of all: one to myself.

HEY THERE, BUDDY,

I'm calling you buddy because I want to be your friend now. For a long time I was my own worst enemy; in fact, I was my only enemy.

It was me that let fear dominate my life. It was me that hung on to past traumas to fill the present with suffering. It was my own voice telling me in my head that I didn't deserve anything good and that I was inferior to other people.

I filled myself with insecurities and doubt, jealousy and resentment. I judged myself and criticized everything I did. I damaged my own health and well-being, and I was responsible for the problems in my life. The solutions and the answers to all this were in me.

I was the accused, the judge, and the hangman in my own life. I handed down the sentences and imposed the punishments.

And yet today I forgive myself for everything, because I realize that I always did the best I could. I understand that I was sensitive and vulnerable, just like all human beings, and that the experiences in my life molded my personality. Today I reject any guilt over my mistakes, because it doesn't help anyone or solve anything.

I was late in learning that I was capable of changing my life, despite my wounds and the situations around me. It took me a long time to understand that I am my own master, that my thoughts determine my existence, that I was not a slave of circumstance and that it was within my power to change, improve, and live in harmony.

Now I can see that my life was marvelous, despite the losses and the traumas that we all share. I'm thankful for the opportunity I had to see, hear, feel, and taste, the opportunity to share my life with others and the opportunity to love those around me.

Today I throw off old resentments against others and against myself.

* Today I break the chains that I bound myself with.
* Today I free myself from fear and guilt.
* Today I forgive myself for all my mistakes.
* Today I admit that no one controls my thoughts.
* Today I admit that no one controls my feelings.
* Today I declare myself free of all my wounds.
* Today is a good day to die.
* I love me,
* The most important person in my life.

When I finished writing these letters in my mind, I felt a tremendous sense of release.

"The decision to free yourself from guilt and resentment has more to do with you than with other people," commented my guide. "When you decide to forgive someone, it is you who is freed and who throws off the heavy burden of bitterness. Many people carry baggage on their back their whole life. Their baggage is full of past offenses, animosities, guilt, resentment, wounds, lost loves, disillusionment, broken hearts, infidelities, and misery …"

People say we all have a cross to bear, I interrupted.

"Where did they get that idea? They put their own cross on their backs by holding on to the past, and it's their decision to put it down whenever they want. Nobody asked them to suffer."

They say we have to pay for what we get, I went on.

"That's even worse!!! Who are they supposed to pay? And is it really necessary to pay with suffering? People forget that life is generous with its children and that the love they receive is unconditional. It's given without expecting anything in return, in the same way that plants, animals, and all the other creatures in the world receive everything they need."

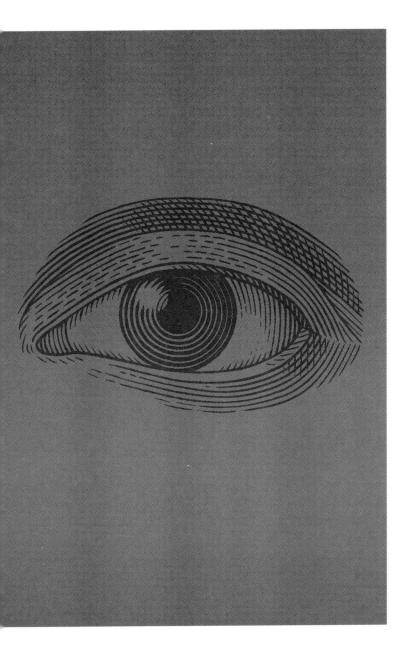

CHAPTER XII

ONCE AGAIN THE NURSE MY EXECUTIONER CAME INTO THE ROOM. FOR THE FIRST TIME, SHE CAME OVER TO LOOK AT ME. SHE BENT DOWN UNTIL HER FACE WAS A FEW INCHES FROM MINE. SHE LOOKED STRAIGHT INTO MY EYES LIKE SOMEONE PEERING THROUGH A WINDOW. HER FEATURES WERE COARSE AND HER SKIN WAS WRINKLED AND COVERED IN POCKMARKS. HER LIPS WERE THIN, COLORLESS, AND LIFELESS. SHE HAD A HORRIBLE WART ON HER FOREHEAD WITH TWO THICK HAIRS GROWING OUT OF IT THAT MADE IT LOOK EVEN MORE DISGUSTING. HER BREATH WAS RANK AND HEAVY, AND WHEN SHE EXHALED SHE MADE A STRANGE, UNPLEASANT WHEEZING SOUND.

She looked at me like that for several seconds and I saw my own face reflected in her dark eyes. At that moment I understood something very important: this woman was a different version of me! We both had the capacity to hurt others, the capacity to lie, to be greedy, to be selfish, and even to kill. The realization sent a shiver through me.

"Don't be so surprised," said my guide when he noticed my reaction. "This is part of the freedom that you've been given and part of your nature. To be free, you need options. What merit would a person who was fair to others have if he had no choice in the matter? What makes our actions worthy is that we choose what's best for everyone, not just for ourselves."

We choose between good and evil?

"It's not about good and evil, it's about choosing between what helps us and what harms us. The problem is that some people refuse to acknowledge that any harm you cause to someone else sooner or later comes back to get you. Take this woman as an example: what do you think she's doing here, looking at you like this?"

I have no idea. Maybe she came to make fun of me ... I answered hesitantly.

"She's here to assuage her conscience, to convince herself you're not awake. She keeps telling herself that you're not and that she's doing this for the woman who needs the organs, not for the money. Her main aim is to obtain a benefit, not to harm you."

And yet she'll be tormented by uncertainty for a long time.

"Right, and that's the decision she's taken. She's exercising her freedom."

The nurse put one hand over my face, distracting me, as if she couldn't stand to have me watch, and I heard the click of the third switch being turned off.

This time I felt the change in my stomach. It was as if all of a sudden I was very hungry. Then I felt a tingling sensation from my waist to my toes. Exhaustion overwhelmed me and I blacked out.

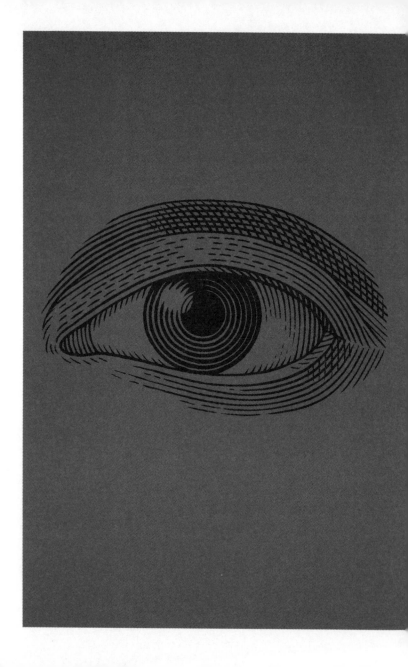

CHAPTER XIII

A PLEASANT SENSATION ON MY CHEEKS REVIVED ME. SLOWLY I FOCUSED MY EYES AND SAW MY LITTLE SISTER GRACE, PLAYFULLY STROKING MY FACE WITH HER HANDS AND SAYING,

"Wake up, sleepyhead! Come on, wake up, you've got an important visitor."

I was slightly taken aback to see her, because my parents had wanted to spare her the distress of seeing me like this and hadn't let her come.

I noticed that only one of the switches was still on, so the nurse must have turned off the other two while I was unconscious.

"Your baby's been born—a beautiful little girl! Wake up and take a look at her. Wake up! Wake up!"

Grace started to shout and I could hear desperation in her voice.

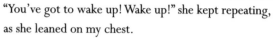

"You've got to wake up! Wake up!" she kept repeating, as she leaned on my chest.

"You see, that's why we didn't want you to come here," said my mother, standing right behind her with my baby in her arms. "Try to calm down, honey."

"Come on over here, baby. It's okay, take it easy," my father said.

He was standing next to her and he bent down to take her by the shoulders and gently lead her out of the room.

Grace began to relax a little and my mother turned to me, bent over slightly, and pulled back the blanket that was covering my baby's face. She said,

"Look, here's your little girl …"

Her eyes were closed, her face red and puffy, and she had one hand resting on her cheek. My heart swelled as I looked at her sleeping obliviously. She was the most beautiful thing I had ever set eyes on.

Suddenly the hateful nurse came in, surely to turn off the last of the switches.

"What's going on here?" she yelled, obviously afraid that she had been found out.

"We just came in to show him the baby," said my

mother uneasily.

"You can't be here! You've got to go!" shouted the nurse, pushing my mother away from me. "Get out, right now!" She was frantic, afraid her plans were falling apart.

You can't do this! I begged her in my head. *Just let me look at my baby for a few more seconds, please!* I was beside myself; the happiest moment of my life—the last moment of my life—was being taken away from me. *Just a few more seconds! I just want to touch her one time!!!* Suddenly Grace screamed from her place by the door, where she had been watching what was happening. "He moved!"

My mother and the nurse turned to look at me and saw that my left arm was raised, as if I wanted to reach out to my baby. The nurse was so shocked that in her hurry to get out of the room as fast as possible she knocked over the drip by my bed and the glass bottle shattered, sending saline solution over the floor. She pushed past my father and Grace and ran out in a panic.

"Call the doctor!" said my mother to my father, who was staring at me astonished.

I brought my left hand to the tube in my mouth and tugged at it desperately to try to remove it. I felt that I was choking.

"Wait a minute, honey, the doctor's on his way," said
my mother, putting one hand on my shoulder and
holding the baby in her other arm.

Almost immediately my father arrived with the doctor who had
saved my life the first time. When he saw me lifting my head
from the pillow, he came over and put his hand on my forehead
to calm me down. He removed two elastic bands running from
my mouth behind my head and slowly but deftly took out the
plastic tube that was blocking my throat.

I breathed in a huge lungful of air and for the first time
closed my eyes. When I breathed out I coughed a little, then
began to cry uncontrollably.

"Please, could we have a moment?" said the doctor
to my parents and Grace, who were crowding around
my bed.
"Come on, sweetheart. Let's let the doctor do his job,"
said my father to my mother, motioning for them to
leave the room.
"Will he be okay, doctor?" asked my mother anxiously.
"He's awake," said the doctor. "That's all we know
right now. Please, go and take this baby back to the
maternity ward."

"Thank God," said my mother emotionally.

"I told you! I knew he was gonna wake up!" Grace said happily as the three of them left the room.

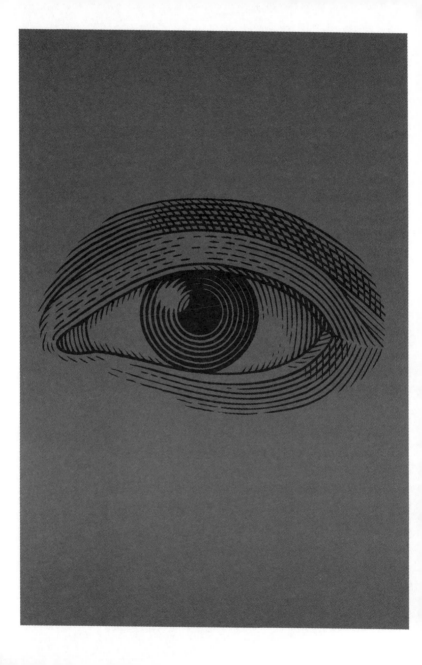

CHAPTER XIV

THE NEXT DAY I HAD SURGERY TO REMOVE THE STOMACH TUBE THAT THE DOCTORS HAD PUT IN ME AND I WAS MOVED TO ANOTHER ROOM IN THE CONVALESCENT WARD.

Ironically the same nurse who had tried to kill me was now assigned to look after me. When she came into my room she was scared to death.

"Good morning," she said nervously, looking at the floor.

"Good morning," I replied as naturally as possible.

"Here's your medicine," she said, leaving a pair of pills on my bedside table. She checked that everything was in order in the room, while I followed her around with my eyes.

"Well, I'll be leaving now," she said jumpily. "If you need anything you can call me with this button."

She hesitated and I sensed that she wanted to find out how much I knew about what had happened.

"Thank you, that's kind of you!" I replied, pretending that everything was okay.

She headed toward the door and was about to leave the room when I asked her:

"By the way … what happened to the woman who needed my kidneys?"

As the realization dawned on her that I knew everything, her face went as white as a sheet. She stared at me as if she had seen a ghost.

"The wo … woman? Fine. She's fine. She found a donor the same day that you woke up," she said, stuttering and visibly panicked.

She said nothing more and left, closing the door behind her. I later found out that she and the doctor who had planned to sell my organs both left their jobs that same day, evidently afraid that I would report them. Nobody heard from them again.

I will never forget the next day my family came to see me. My mother was so excited she ran into the room and gave me a bear hug, then took my face in her hands and smothered me in kisses.

"It's a miracle! I'm so happy to see you looking well again!" she said between tears and kisses.

"Mom, I wanted to hug you so badly! I really love you,"

I answered, putting my arm around her shoulders with tears streaming down my face.

My father stood watching us, trying to hold back his own tears.

"Come here, Dad. You don't have to hide anything.
I know you have feelings too and you love me as much
as I love you," I said, holding out my arms to him.

He came over to the bed and the three of us spent a long time just hugging and crying together.

After that my brother and sisters came in to see me. Everyone was amazed to hear that I had been conscious the whole time. Grace was so happy when I told her that she had helped me to wake up. She kept fidgeting and holding my hand proudly.

The last one to come in the room was Laura. She was holding our baby girl in her arms. Everyone else decided to leave and give us some time alone.

"Hi, sweetheart. How are you?" she asked quietly.
"I'm alive, thanks to you and that baby you're carrying."
"Thanks to us?"
"Yeah. It was only because of you that I held on to life
so hard. I wanted so badly to meet our daughter that
it gave me strength."

"Well, here she is," she said, holding out the baby to me. Gingerly I took her in my arms and held her against my chest. I was mesmerized by the way she opened and closed her little mouth.

"She looks like you," said Laura smiling gently. She leaned over and kissed me on the lips.

We stayed together for a while, and then Laura went to rest because she was still recovering from the birth.

That afternoon I felt like the luckiest guy alive. I had been reborn and now I had the opportunity to start my life over again, to start a family, and to put into practice all the things I'd learned in the past nine months.

I gave thanks for my good luck to God, life, nature, and the entire universe. There was no doubt in my mind that I was a part of everything that exists.

I closed my eyes and thought of my guide. I called him, mentally and out loud.

"Guide, my friend, I want to talk with you." I tried several times but got no reply.

I was sad to think that he would no longer be with me, that I would no longer be able to learn from him.

That night, just as I was falling asleep, I heard his voice sounding very far away. He said,

"I can't go anywhere because I'm part of you. I'll be here when you need me ..."

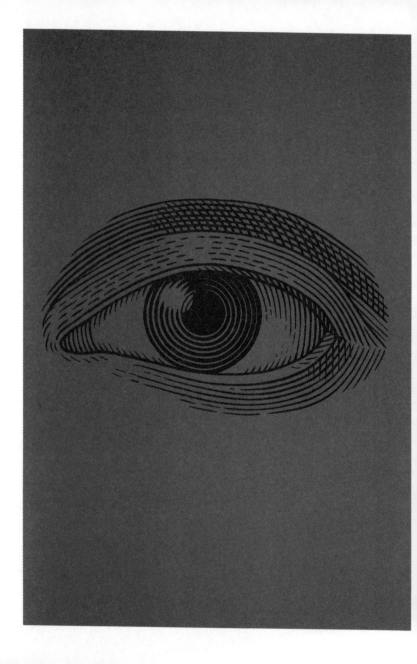

CHAPTER XV

I SPENT TWO MORE WEEKS IN THE HOSPITAL, RECUPERATING AND GETTING VISITS FROM DOCTORS WHO WERE INTERESTED IN MY CASE.

When the time was nearing for me to be discharged, I started asking everyone I could about Faith. I wanted to thank her for her kindness and for taking care of me. I got the same reply over and over again: "No one called Faith has ever worked at this hospital." Not even my family remembered having met her.

Her presence in my life will always remain a mystery to me.

Despite spending three months in physical therapy, I was never able to fully recover all my mobility. I walk with a cane because I have a slight limp in my left leg, and I can't move my right arm much. None of this is a problem for me; the sheer joy of being able to communicate with people and participate in life is so great that these little defects are unimportant.

Laura and I got married and are happy living together with our little girl in a modest apartment. Our lives took on new meaning and we now enjoy the simplest of things.

One day I decided to share what I had learned through this experience, and I began to write the book you are now holding.

I want to ask you, my dear friend, my brother, my sister:

What are you a slave to? To wounds you received as a child? To childhood traumas? To what someone else decided you should be? To an unfulfilling relationship? To a job you don't like? To the routine of your life?

Free yourself! Toss the baggage off your back, where you keep your resentment, regrets, and guilt. Stop blaming other people and your past for things that don't go right in your life. Every day you have the chance to start over. Every morning when you open your eyes, you are reborn and get another chance to change the things you don't like and improve your life. It is all up to you. Your happiness doesn't depend on your parents, your partner, your friends, or your past. It only depends on you.

What holds you back? Fear of rejection? Of success? Of failure? Of what people will say? Of criticism? Of making a mistake? Of being alone?

Break the chains you have bound yourself with! The only thing you should be afraid of is not being yourself, of letting your life go by without doing what you want, of failing to take advantage of this opportunity to show yourself to other people, to say what you think, to share what you have. You are part of life and, like everyone else, you can hold your head high. The errors of the past are forgotten and the errors of the future will be forgiven. No one is keeping a record of your failings, except you. The judge who sternly rebukes you, the executioner who punishes you, the bad friend who criticizes you, is you! Give yourself a break. Forgive yourself: only you can.

When are you going to tell the people you love how much you care about them? When you only have a few moments left to live? When they only have a few moments left to live?

The love you don't express today is lost forever. Remember that life is so short and so fragile that we have no time to waste on being bitter or on stupid arguments. Today is the day to forgive past offenses and iron out old quarrels. Give yourself to the people you love, but don't expect them to change. Love them for what they are and respect the most valuable gift you and they have been given: freedom.

Enjoy your relationships without making a fuss. If you try to make everyone do as you want or be as you want them to be, if you try to control the people around you, you'll fill your life with conflict. Let other people make their own decisions, just as you must make your own with the aim of achieving what's best for all. In this way you will fill your life with harmony.

Finally, what are you waiting for to start enjoying life? For all your problems to be resolved? For your traumas to disappear? For someone finally to recognize your worth? For love to come into your life? For someone who left to come back? For everything to turn out just as you want? For the economic recession to be over? For a miracle to happen? For everything to magically be beautiful and perfect?

Wake up, brother! Wake up, sister! This is life! Life isn't what happens when all your plans pan out, or when you finally have that thing you want so badly. Life is what's happening at this very moment. Your life right now is you reading this paragraph, wherever you happen to be and in the circumstances that surround you at this moment. Right now your heart is carrying blood to all the cells in your body and your lungs are making sure that oxygen gets to where it needs to be. At this moment, something we don't understand is keeping you alive and allowing you to see, think, express yourself, move, laugh, and even cry if you want to!

Don't take life for granted. Don't get used to waking up every day and being bored, bad-tempered, or worried. Open your eyes and give thanks for the miracle you have the ability to see. Give thanks for your ability to hear the birds singing or your children laughing. Put your hands on your chest and feel your heart beating strong, telling you:

"You're alive, you're alive, you're alive."

I know life isn't perfect and that it's full of difficult situations. Maybe that's how it's supposed to be. Maybe that's why you've been given all the tools you need to face it: tears to mourn loss, words to share love, arms to give hugs, hands to help others, a heart to receive love and share love, a mind that lets you choose your responses to whatever happens.

I also know that you aren't perfect. Nobody is. And yet, millions of different variables came together so you can exist. You were formed according to an amazing design and you share your virtues and defects with the rest of humanity.

Share your passions, your fears, your wounds, your weaknesses, your secrets, and your love with all your brothers and sisters. Welcome to the human race! And remember, so-called defects are part of your freedom, part of your humanity, when you recognize them.

If you're asking yourself who I am to tell you all this, I'm nobody. I'm just a different version of who you are. Another human being among billions of human beings. But one who has decided to be free and to take back control of his life.

I hope you do, too.

HAY HOUSE

Look within

Join the conversation about latest products,
events, exclusive offers and more.

f Hay House UK

🐦 @HayHouseUK

📷 @hayhouseuk

❤ healyourlife.com

We'd love to hear from you!